This Calendar

BELONGS TO THE
KIND-HEARTED...

....

....

BY DOING SIMPLE ACTS OF *Kindness* FOR OTHERS WE CAN'T HELP

BUT LIFT OURSELVES UP, TOO

Christmas is the Season for giving.

How wonderful to teach young children about the benefits of kindness and making the world a better place because they are in it.

Perhaps make this book a family tradition that can be passed on to each generation.

Make memories that will fill your child's heart with Joy.

As an extra special bonus, hidden in each picture is Crackers the Christmas Cat.
Can you help find him?

Be a Happiness Hero/ine

You may not know, but small things that you do, can make a huge difference to someones life

Why not leave a kind note in a
Library book or donate
a pile of your
old comics to a
Dr's Surgery or friend

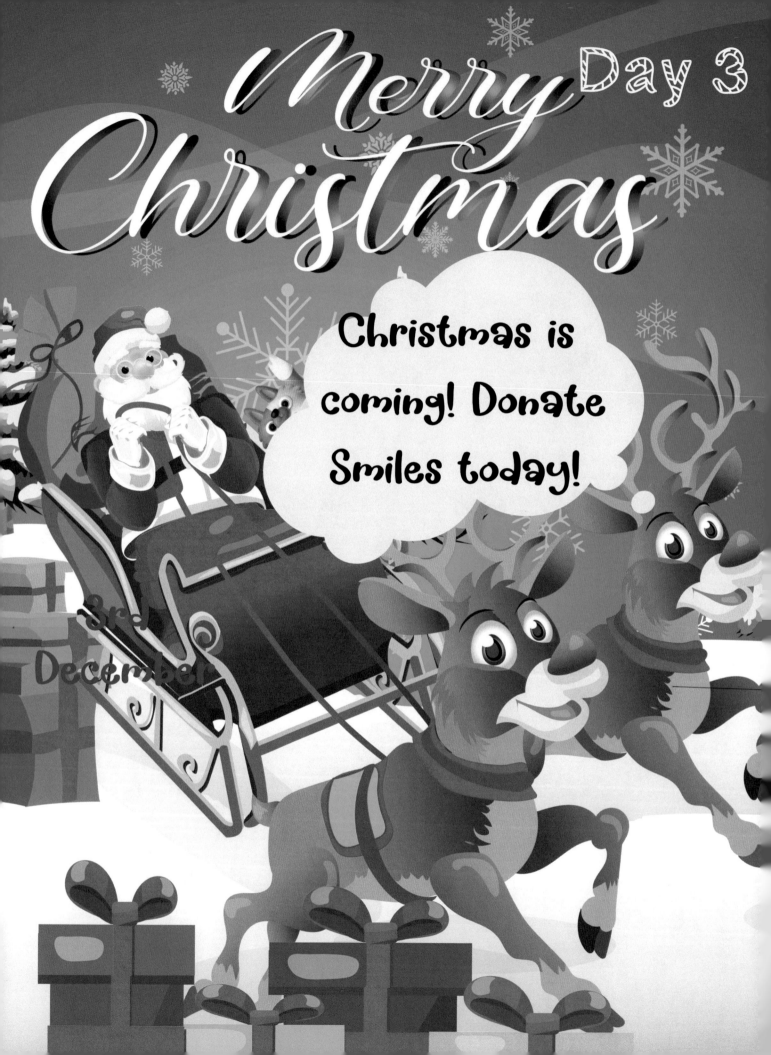

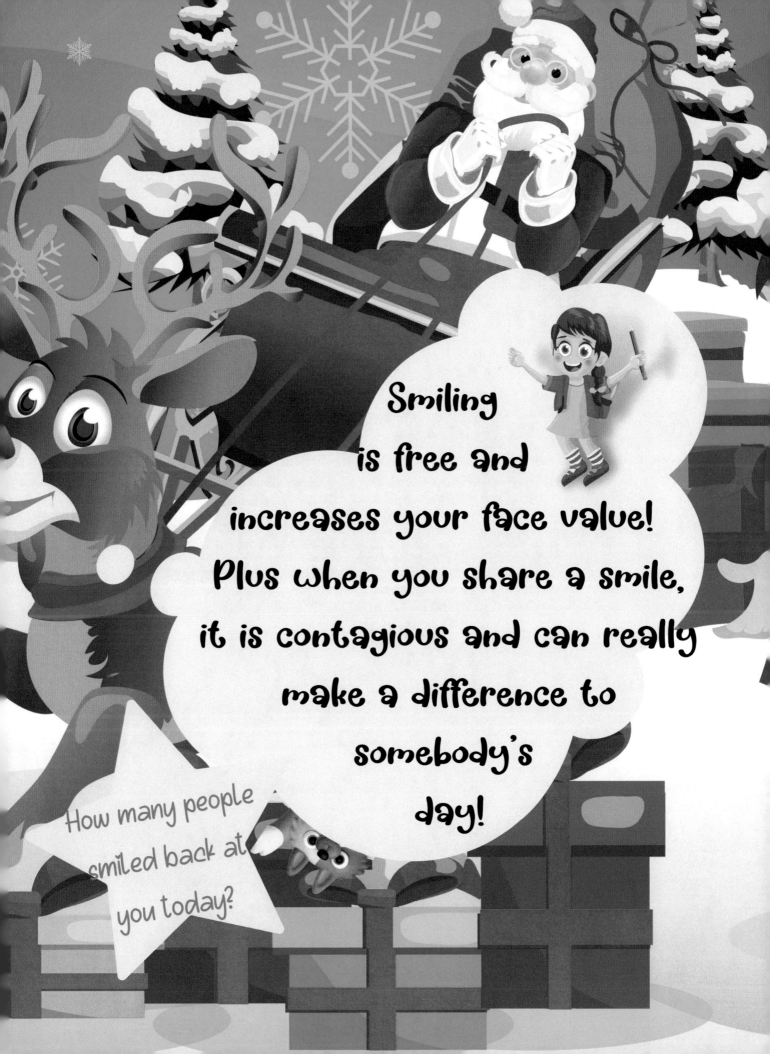

Smiling is free and increases your face value! Plus when you share a smile, it is contagious and can really make a difference to somebody's day!

How many people smiled back at you today?

Day 4

Be really helpful and tidy your toys or bedroom without being asked

4th December

Day 5

Fill a 'Kindness Jar' with candy for a family

OR

Share some of your candy/sweets with a friend at school

And you'll also be kinder to your teeth!

5th December

Day 7
Make a thank you sign
for the postperson
or delivery driver
LOVE
MAIL
7th
December

Draw a picture of your favourite things with a Big THANK YOU! And put it where the delivery folks can see it!

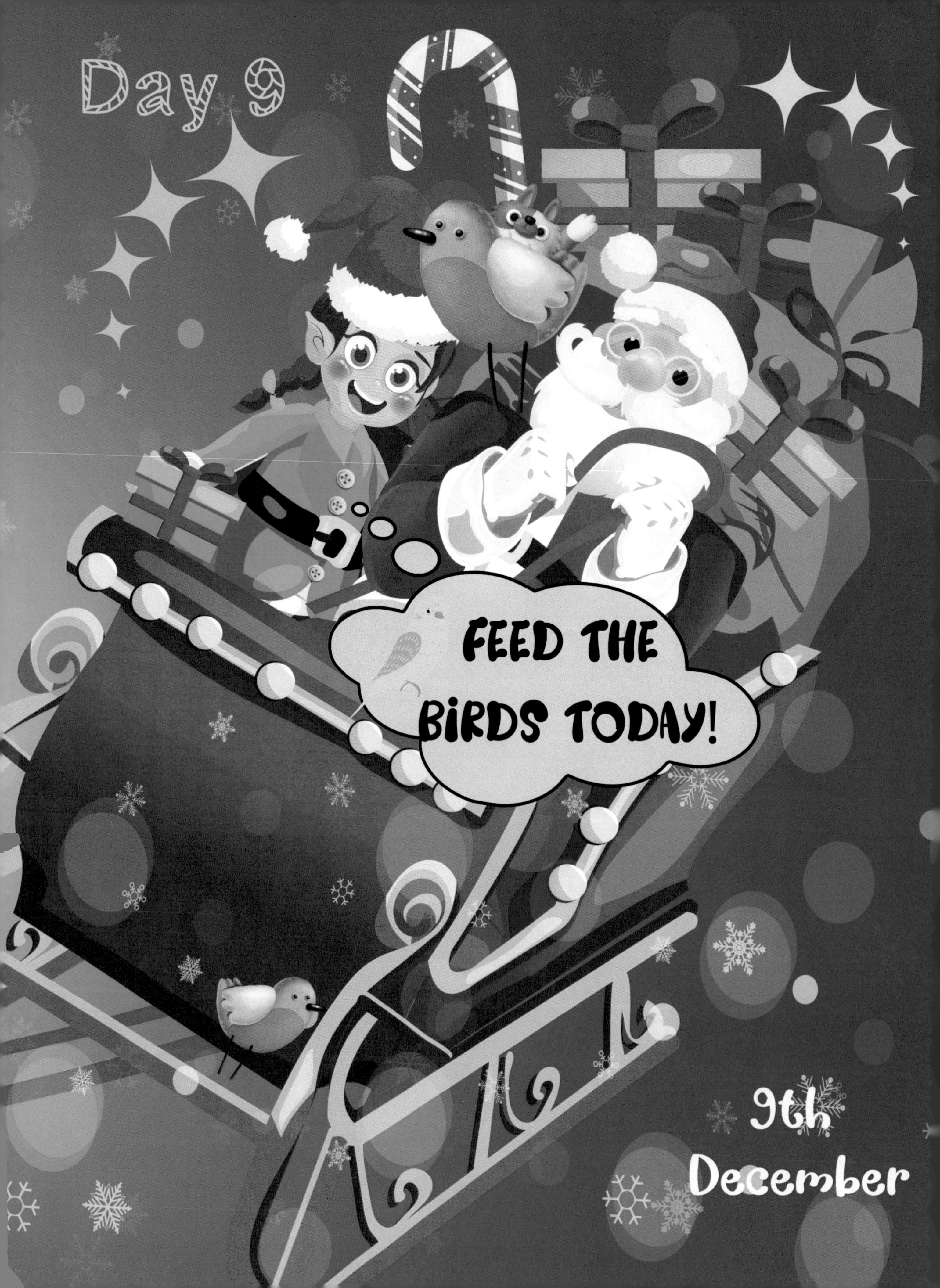
Day 9
FEED THE BIRDS TODAY!
9th December

Birds need high-fat foods
during the winter to keep their
fat reserves to
survive the frosty nights.
Save your bacon rinds and suggest making
fat balls for them at school or
with an older brother
or sister.

Day 11

DONATE THIS WEEKS POCKET MONEY TO CHARITY

11th December

Day 12
ENCOURAGE SOMEONE
Tell someone what they really do well..
Your Ski-ing Rocks!!
12th December

This is such a busy time
of year
for grown-ups.
Offering to help with tasks
is a way to show you care

Christmas
Scavenger Hunt

Tree ☐

Ornament ☐

Gift ☐

Santa ☐

Wreath ☐

Lights ☐

Stocking ☐

Snowman ☐

Holly ☐

Candy Cane ☐

Day 16

kindness CHANGES everything

Leave kindness stones in the Park

Draw or write some kind words on a stone and leave it for someone to find it!

Delivery folks are very busy.
Bottled water, juice, fruit,
granola bars, make a sign letting
delivery drivers know they're welcome
to take a snack for the road.

Day 19

Help a younger sibling to hang Candy Canes on the tree!

19th December

Day 20

Leave out some

water for the birds

20th
December

Birds need water during winter, but
it can freeze
in the cold weather.
Put the water bowl in a sunny spot or
pop a small ball into the water.
The ball will bob about and help
prevent the water from freezing.

**Day
21**

This Coupon is good for......

This Coupon entitles you to Breakfast in Bed!

This Coupon entitles you to a Free Hug!

This Coupon is good for.....

Day 21

This Coupon entitles you to Breakfast in Bed!

This Coupon entitles you to a Free Hug!

We're getting ready! Are You?

Make a Christmas card for someone you love and tell them what you love about them.

23rd December

Made in the USA
Las Vegas, NV
26 November 2023